Fine-Motor & Scissor Skills

Written by: Aaron Levy & Kelley Wingate Levy
Illustrated by: Karen Sevaly

New York • Toronto • London • Auckland • Sydney
Mexico City • New Delhi • Hong Kong • Buenos Aires

Teaching *Resources*

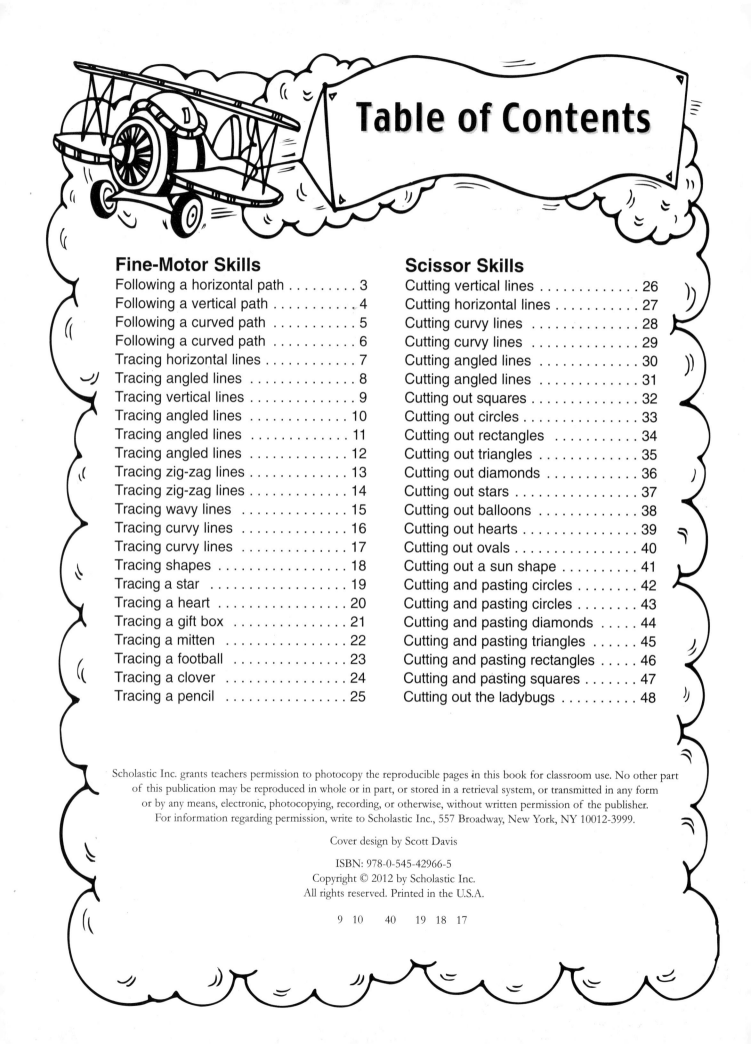

Table of Contents

Fine-Motor Skills

Scissor Skills

Cover design by Scott Davis

ISBN: 978-0-545-42966-5
Copyright © 2012 by Scholastic Inc.
All rights reserved. Printed in the U.S.A.

9   10   40   19 18   17

Name_____

Draw a line to help the runner get to the trophy.

Preschool Basic Skills: Fine-Motor & Scissor Skills
© 2012 by Scholastic Teaching Resources

Name_____

Follow the path to get each bird to its nest.

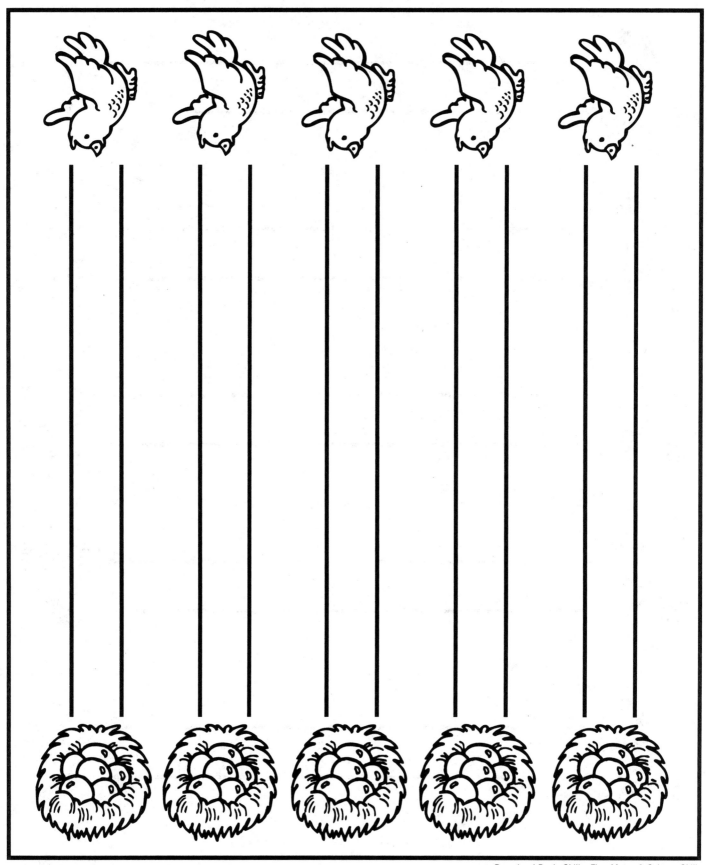

Preschool Basic Skills: Fine-Motor & Scissor Skills
© 2012 by Scholastic Teaching Resources

Name_____

Follow the path to get each dog to its bone.

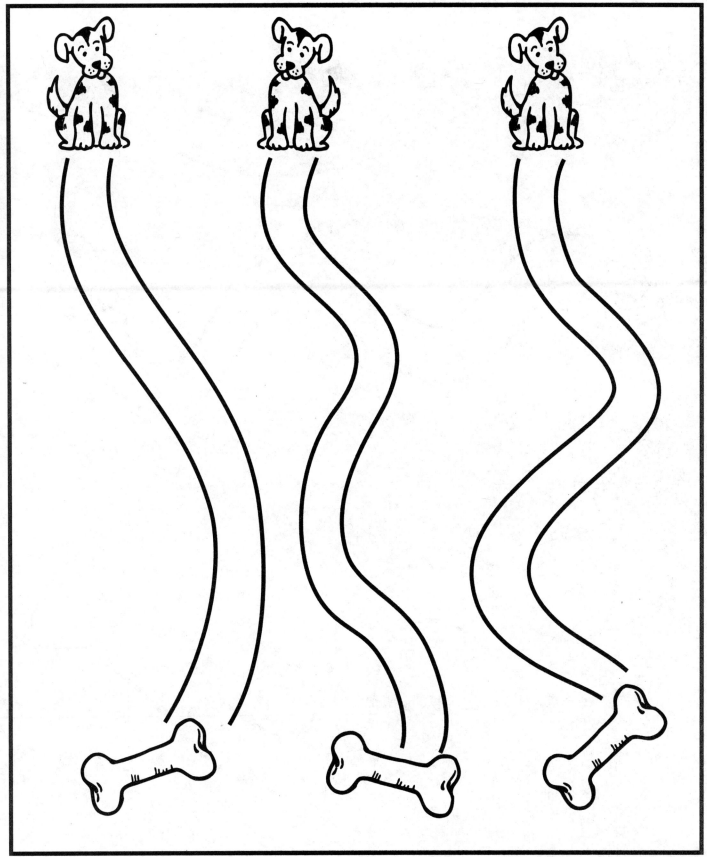

Preschool Basic Skills: Fine-Motor & Scissor Skills
© 2012 by Scholastic Teaching Resources

Follow the path to get each bee to its hive.

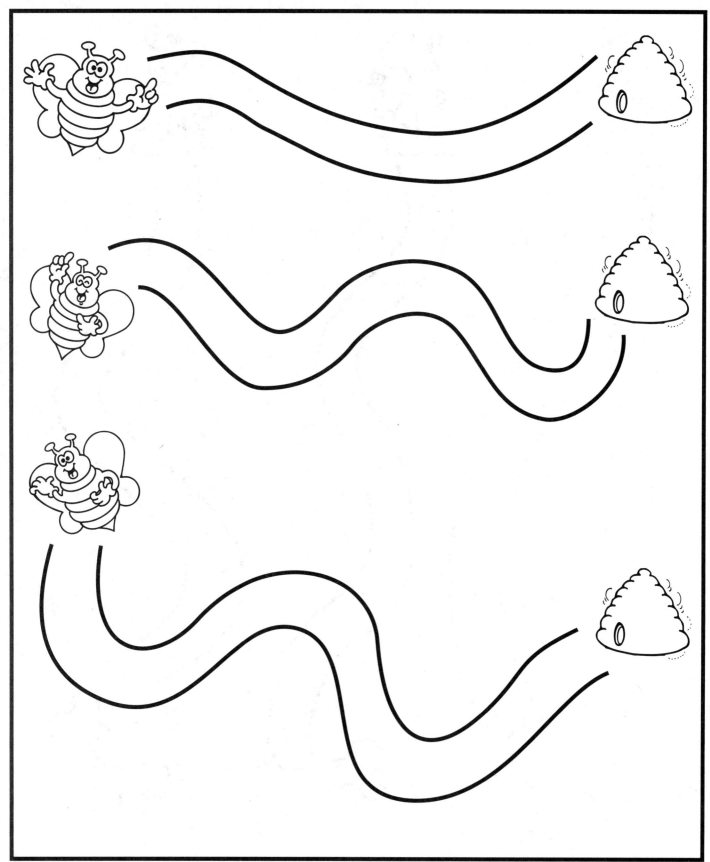

Preschool Basic Skills: Fine-Motor & Scissor Skills
© 2012 by Scholastic Teaching Resources

Name_____

Trace the dotted line to get each butterfly to the flower.

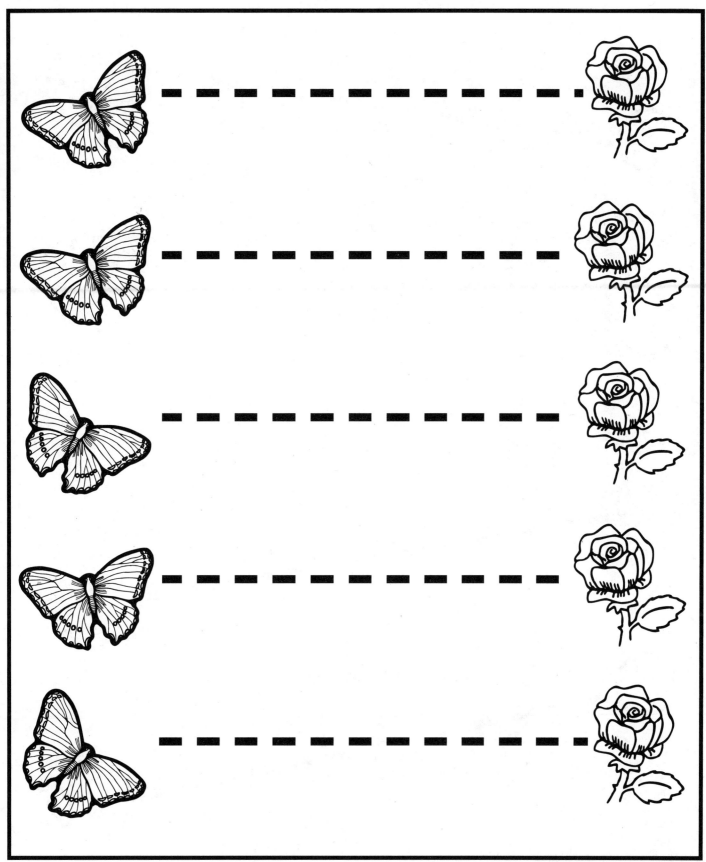

Name_____

Trace the dotted line to get each ball to the mitt.

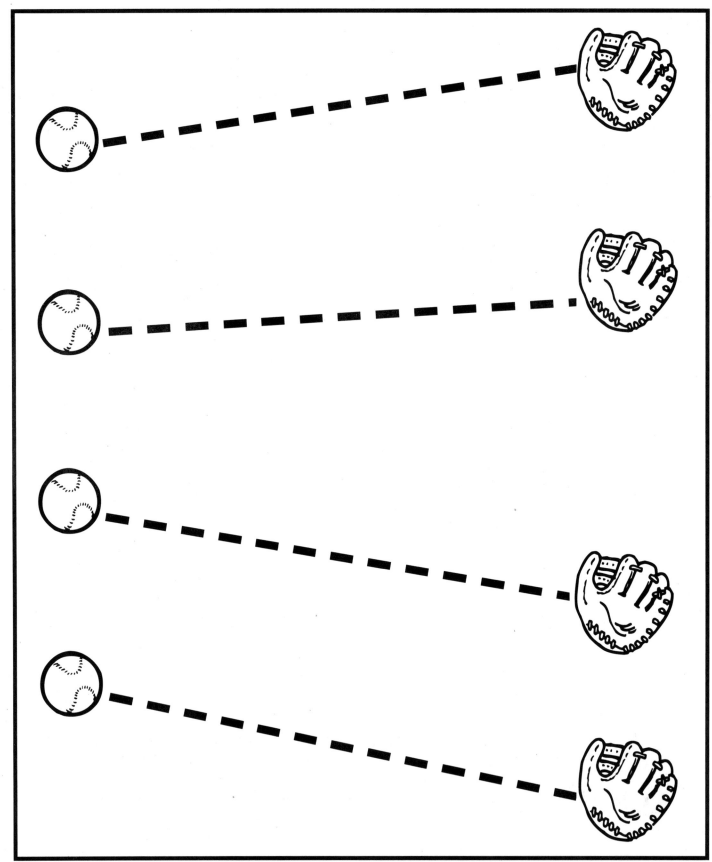

Name_____

Trace the dotted line to help each hammer get to the nail.

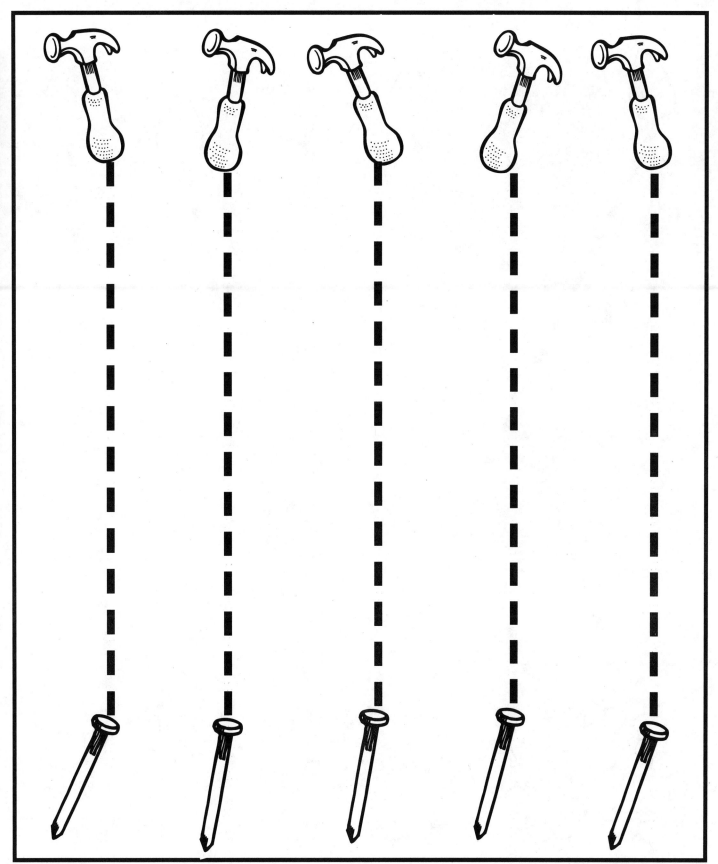

Preschool Basic Skills: Fine-Motor & Scissor Skills
© 2012 by Scholastic Teaching Resources

Trace the dotted lines to get the raindrops to the flowers.

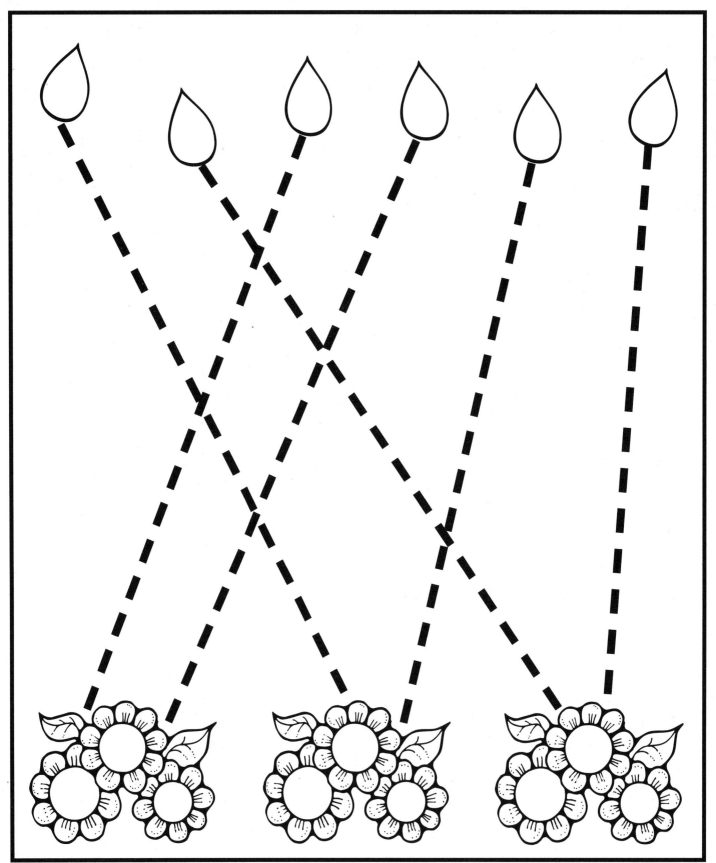

Preschool Basic Skills: Fine-Motor & Scissor Skills
© 2012 by Scholastic Teaching Resources

Name_____

Trace the dotted lines to get the spiders to the webs.

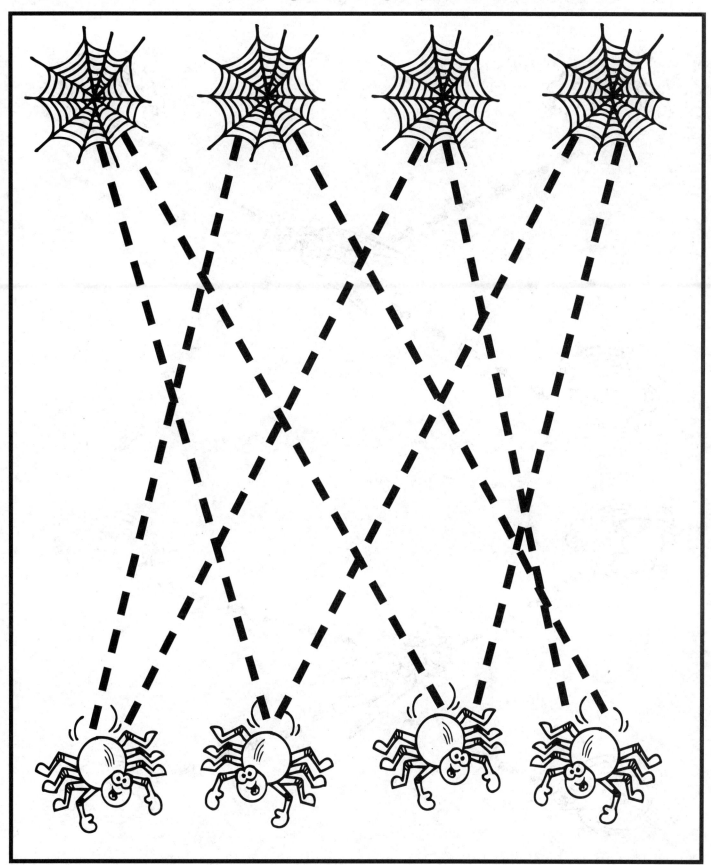

Preschool Basic Skills: Fine-Motor & Scissor Skills
© 2012 by Scholastic Teaching Resources

Trace the dotted lines to get the rabbits to the carrots.

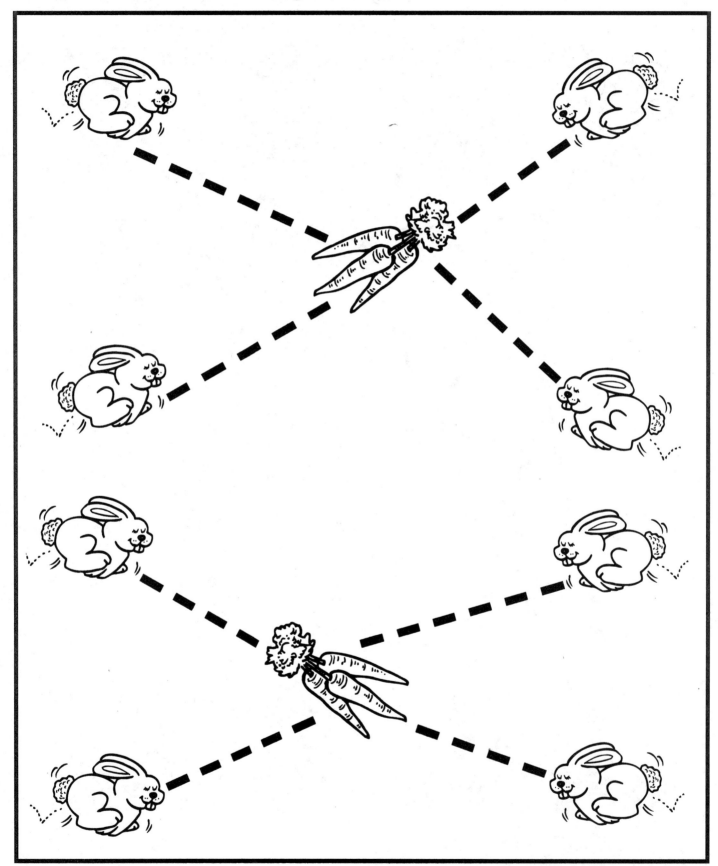

Preschool Basic Skills: Fine-Motor & Scissor Skills
© 2012 by Scholastic Teaching Resources

Name_____

Trace the dotted line to get each toothbrush to the tooth.

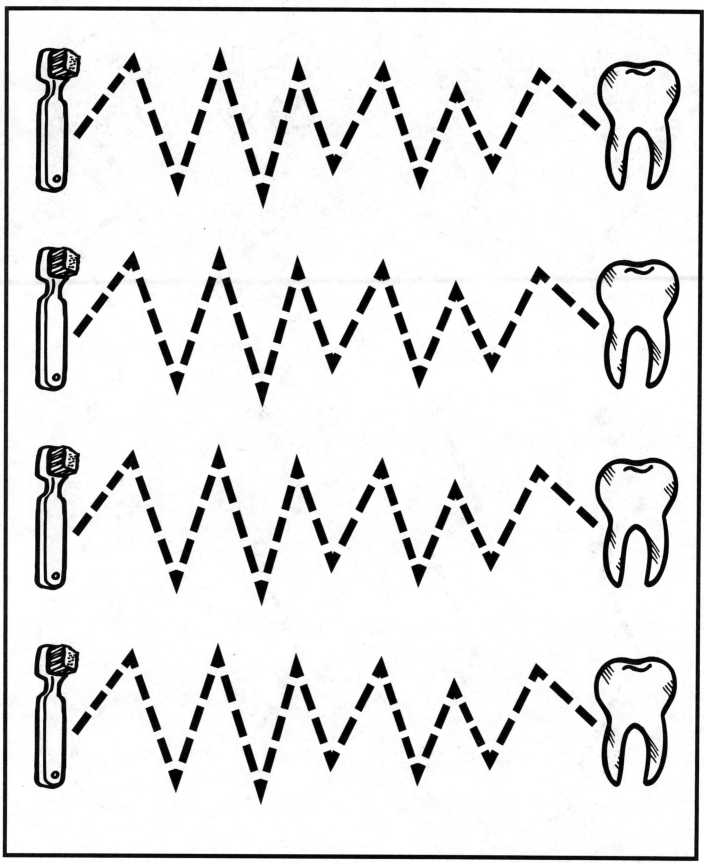

Preschool Basic Skills: Fine-Motor & Scissor Skills
© 2012 by Scholastic Teaching Resources

Trace the dotted line to get each monkey to the banana.

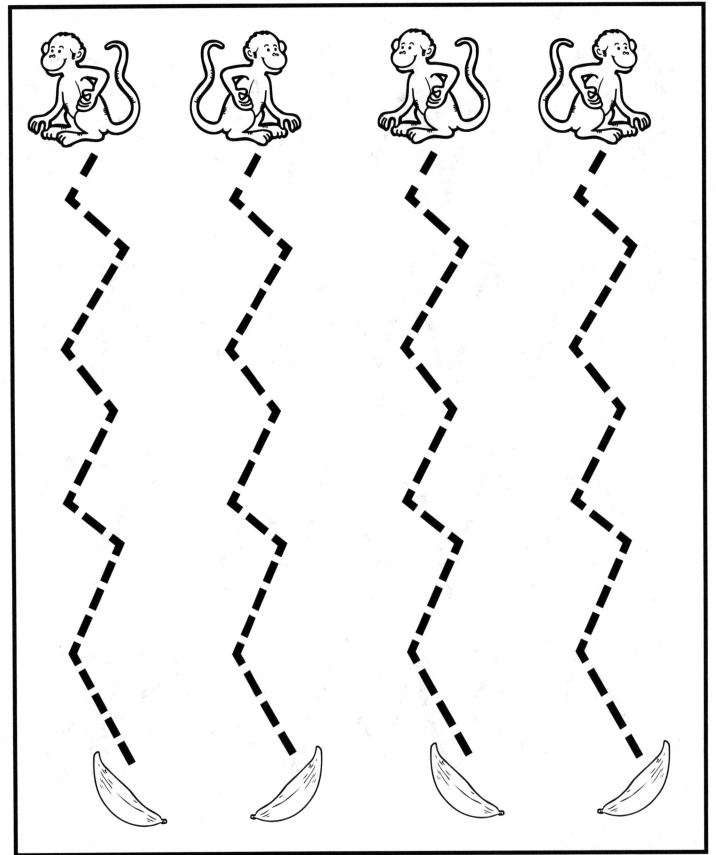

Name_____

Trace the ocean waves. Color the fish.

Preschool Basic Skills: Fine-Motor & Scissor Skills
© 2012 by Scholastic Teaching Resources

Trace the dotted lines to get each kitten to the ball of yarn.

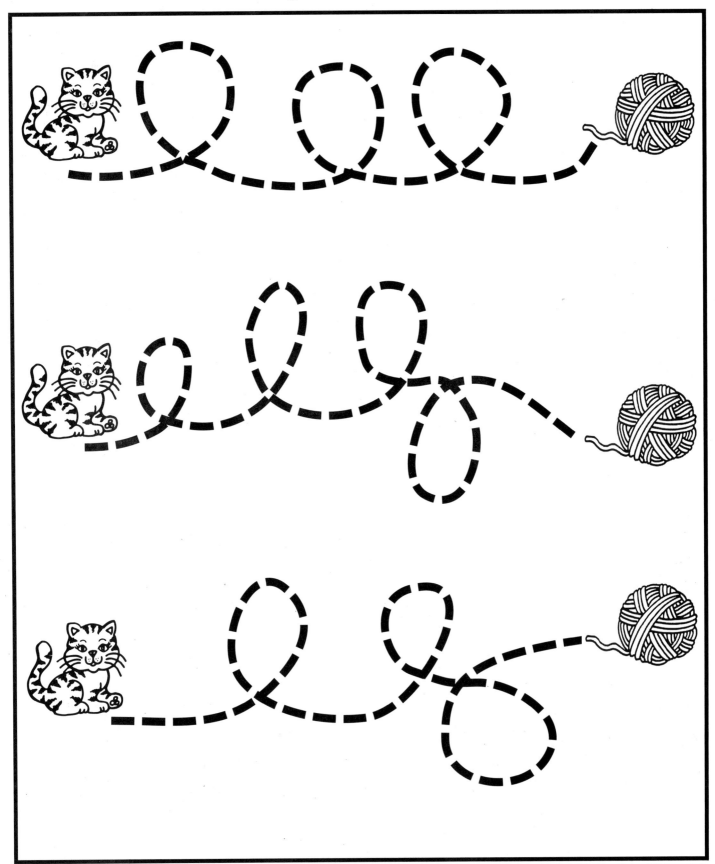

Preschool Basic Skills: Fine-Motor & Scissor Skills
© 2012 by Scholastic Teaching Resources

Name_____

Trace the dotted lines.

Trace and color the shapes.

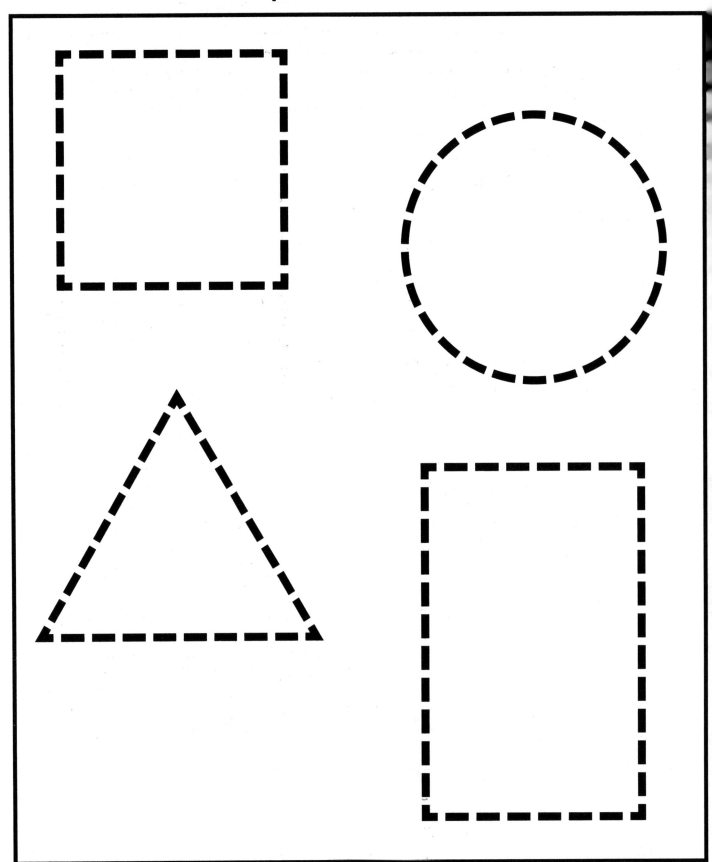

Trace the dotted line to complete the picture.

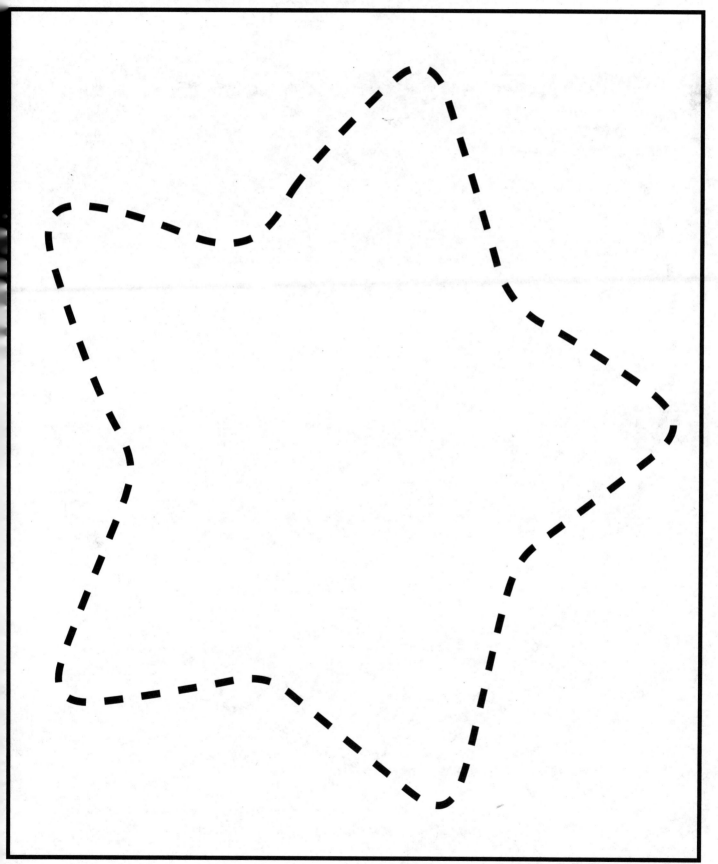

Preschool Basic Skills: Fine-Motor & Scissor Skills
© 2012 by Scholastic Teaching Resources

Name_____

Trace the dotted line to complete the picture.

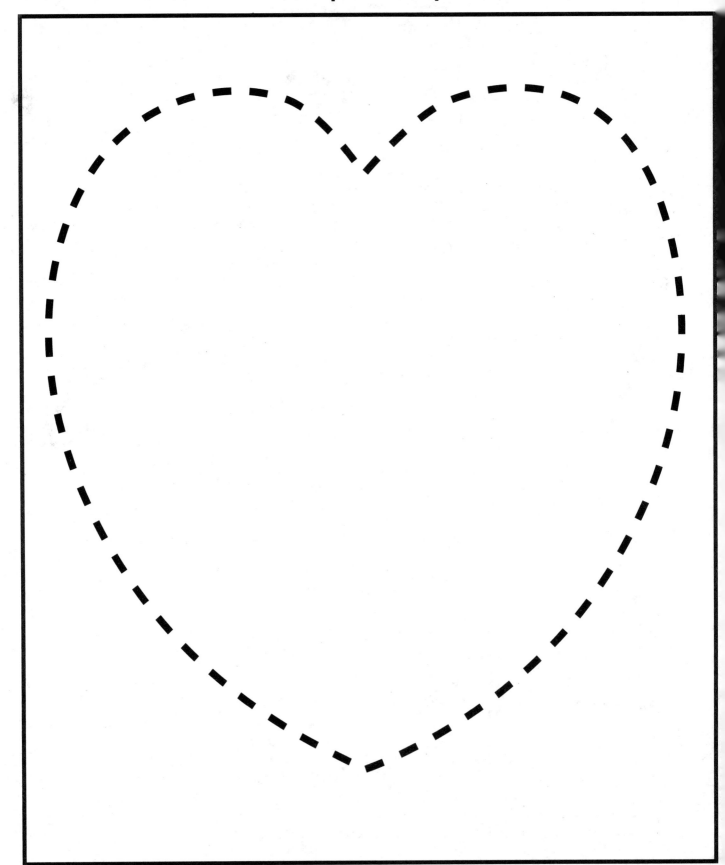

Name_____

Trace the dotted line to complete the picture.

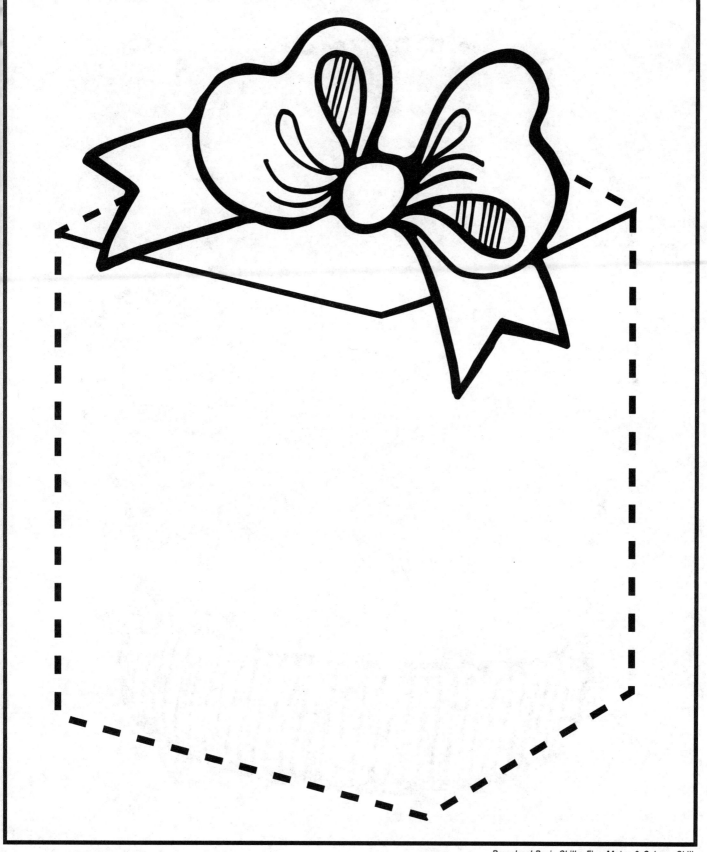

Preschool Basic Skills: Fine-Motor & Scissor Skills

Name_____

Trace the dotted line to complete the picture.

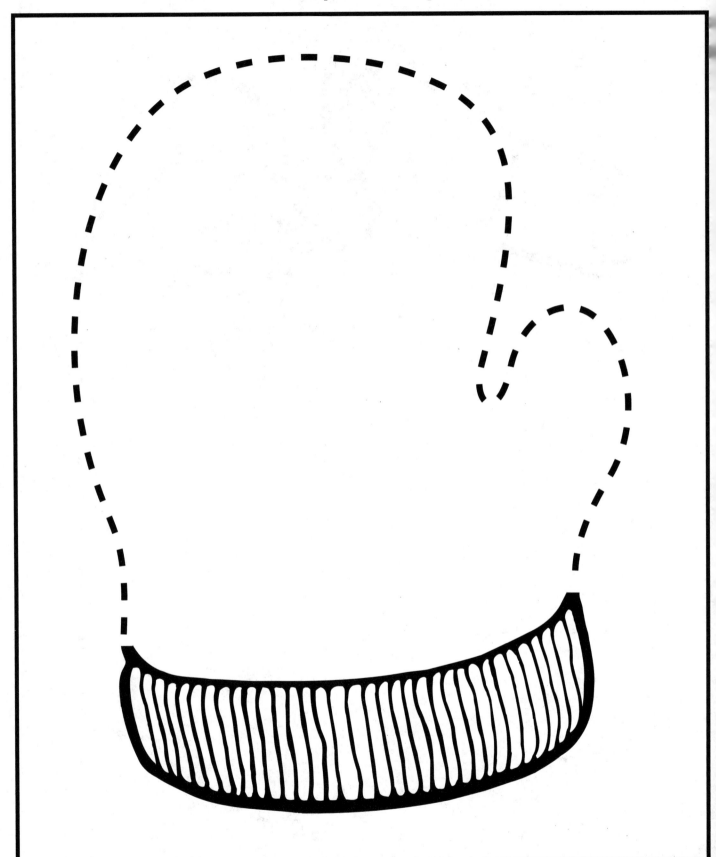

Preschool Basic Skills: Fine-Motor & Scissor Skills
© 2012 by Scholastic Teaching Resources

Trace the dotted line to complete the picture.

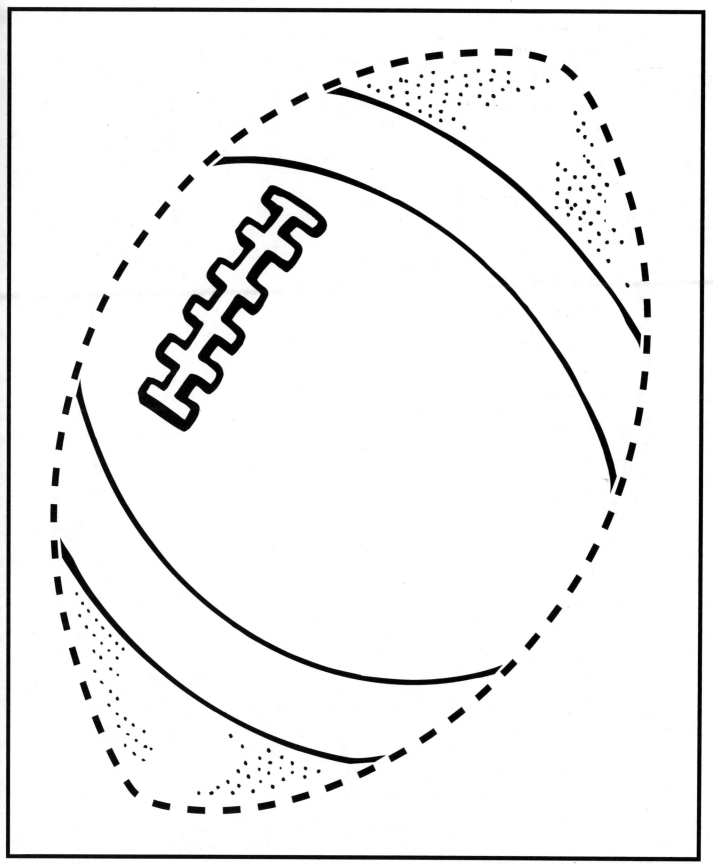

Preschool Basic Skills: Fine-Motor & Scissor Skills
© 2012 by Scholastic Teaching Resources

Name_____

Trace the dotted line to complete the picture.

Preschool Basic Skills: Fine-Motor & Scissor Skills
© 2012 by Scholastic Teaching Resources

Trace the dotted line to complete the picture.

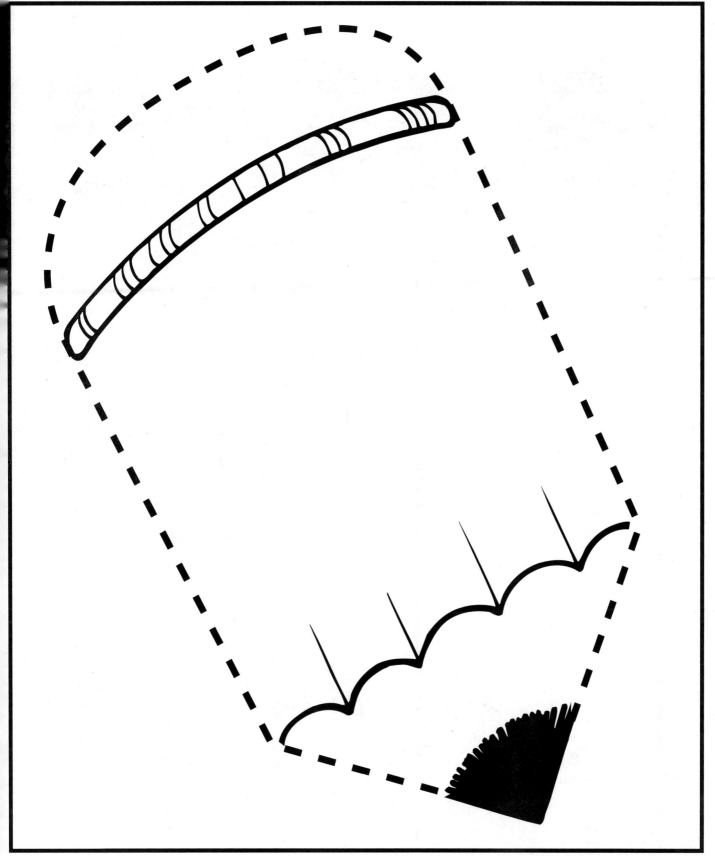

Cut the paths that lead to the fishing poles.

Preschool Basic Skills: Fine-Motor & Scissor Skills

Name_____

Cut the paths that lead to the needles.

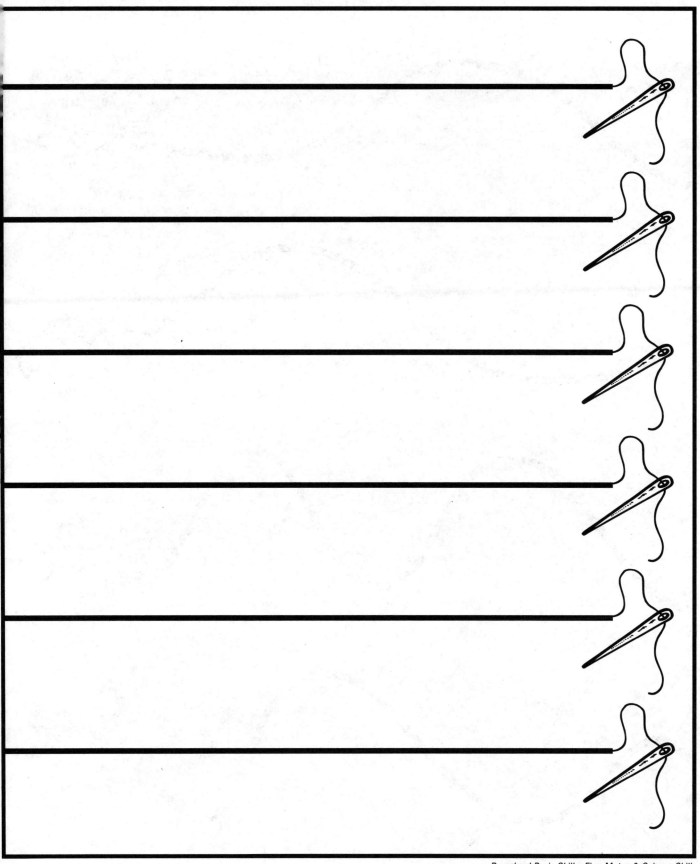

Preschool Basic Skills: Fine-Motor & Scissor Skills
© 2012 by Scholastic Teaching Resources

Name_____

Cut the paths that lead to the fish.

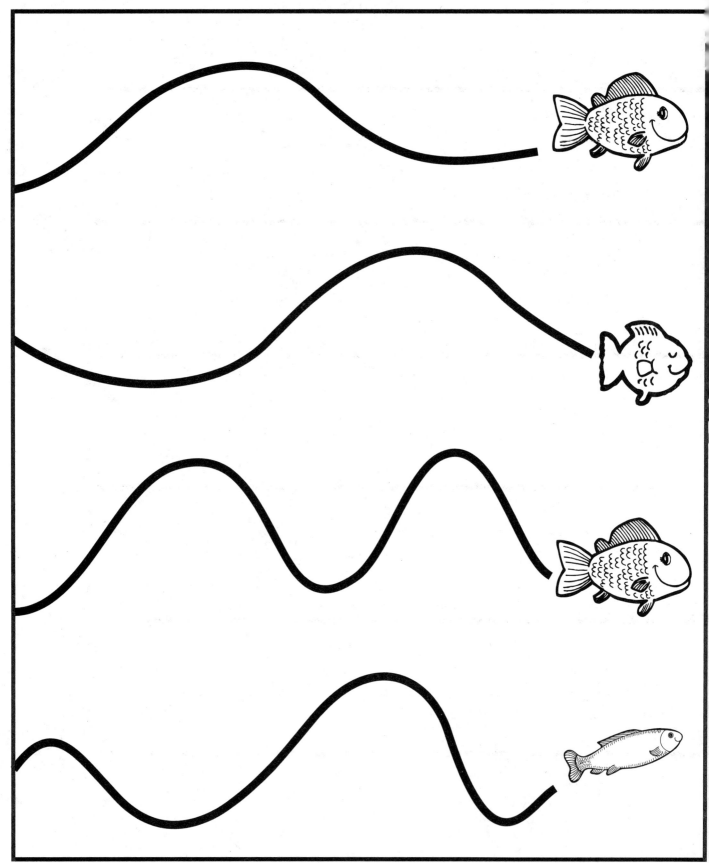

Preschool Basic Skills: Fine-Motor & Scissor Skills
© 2012 by Scholastic Teaching Resources

Name_____

Cut the paths that lead to the kites.

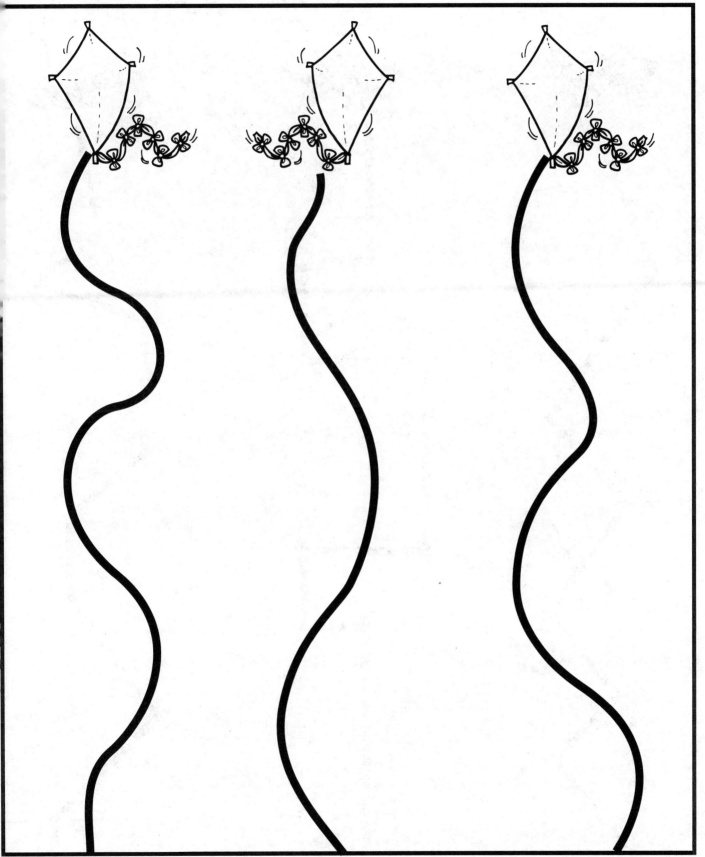

Preschool Basic Skills: Fine-Motor & Scissor Skills

Cut the paths that lead to the grasshoppers.

Preschool Basic Skills: Fine-Motor & Scissor Skills
© 2012 by Scholastic Teaching Resources

Name_____

Cut the paths that lead to the scissors.

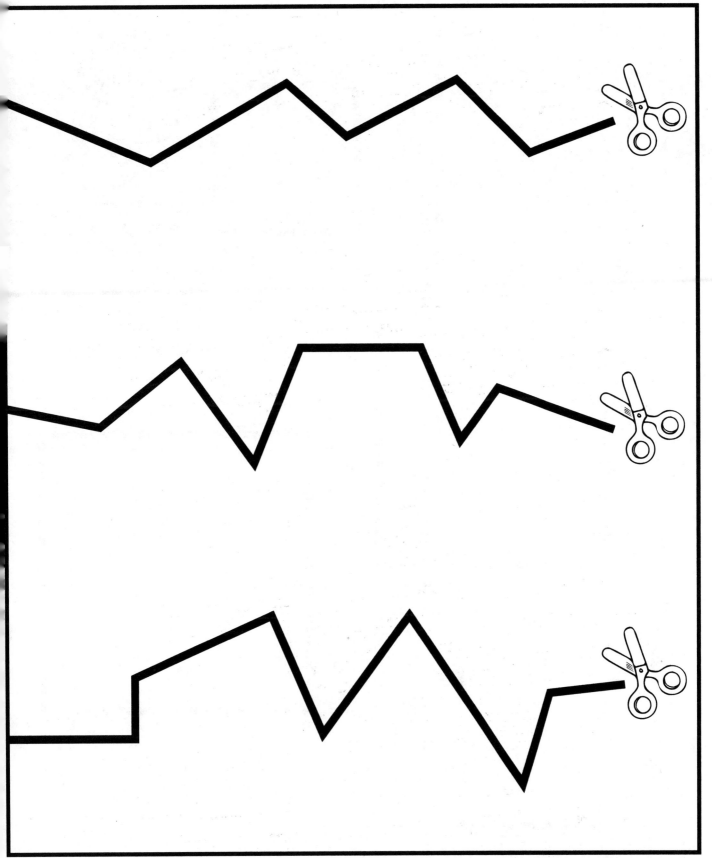

Color each square a different color. Cut out each square.

Preschool Basic Skills: Fine-Motor & Scissor Skills
© 2012 by Scholastic Teaching Resources

Name_____

Color each circle a different color. Cut out each circle.

Preschool Basic Skills: Fine-Motor & Scissor Skills
© 2012 by Scholastic Teaching Resources

Name_____

Color each rectangle a different color. Cut out each rectangle.

Preschool Basic Skills: Fine-Motor & Scissor Skills
© 2012 by Scholastic Teaching Resources

Color each triangle a different color. Cut out each triangle.

Preschool Basic Skills: Fine-Motor & Scissor Skills
© 2012 by Scholastic Teaching Resources

Name_____

Color each diamond a different color. Cut out each diamond.

Color each star a different color. Cut out each star.

Preschool Basic Skills: Fine-Motor & Scissor Skills
© 2012 by Scholastic Teaching Resources

Color each balloon a different color. Cut out each balloon.

Preschool Basic Skills: Fine-Motor & Scissor Skills
© 2012 by Scholastic Teaching Resources

Name_____

Color each heart a different color. Cut out each heart.

Preschool Basic Skills: Fine-Motor & Scissor Skills
© 2012 by Scholastic Teaching Resources

Color each oval a different color. Cut out each oval.

Preschool Basic Skills: Fine-Motor & Scissor Skills
© 2012 by Scholastic Teaching Resources

Color the sun. Cut it out along the solid lines.

Preschool Basic Skills: Fine-Motor & Scissor Skills

Name_____

Trace the shapes along the dotted lines. Color them and cut them out. Paste the shapes into the correct spots.

Preschool Basic Skills: Fine-Motor & Scissor Skills
© 2012 by Scholastic Teaching Resources

Skill: Scissor skills

Trace the shapes along the dotted lines. Color them and cut them out. Paste the shapes into the correct spots.

Preschool Basic Skills: Fine-Motor & Scissor Skills
© 2012 by Scholastic Teaching Resources

Name_____

Trace the shapes along the dotted lines. Color them and cut them out. Paste the shapes into the correct spots.

Preschool Basic Skills: Fine-Motor & Scissor Skills
© 2012 by Scholastic Teaching Resources

Trace the shapes along the dotted lines. Color them and cut them out. Paste the shapes into the correct spots.

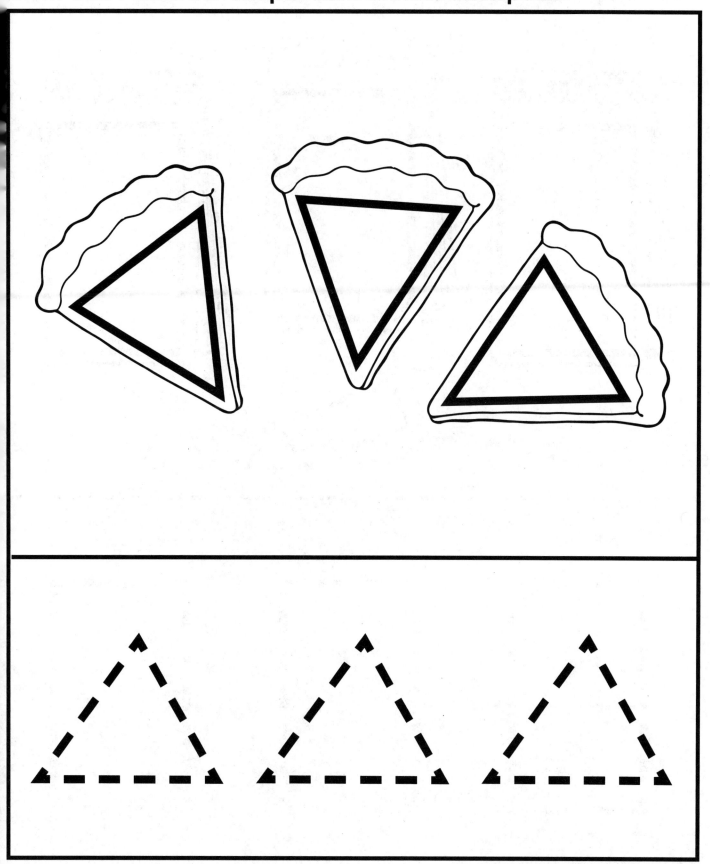

Preschool Basic Skills: Fine-Motor & Scissor Skills
© 2012 by Scholastic Teaching Resources

Name_____

Trace the shapes along the dotted lines. Color them and cut them out. Paste the shapes into the correct spots.

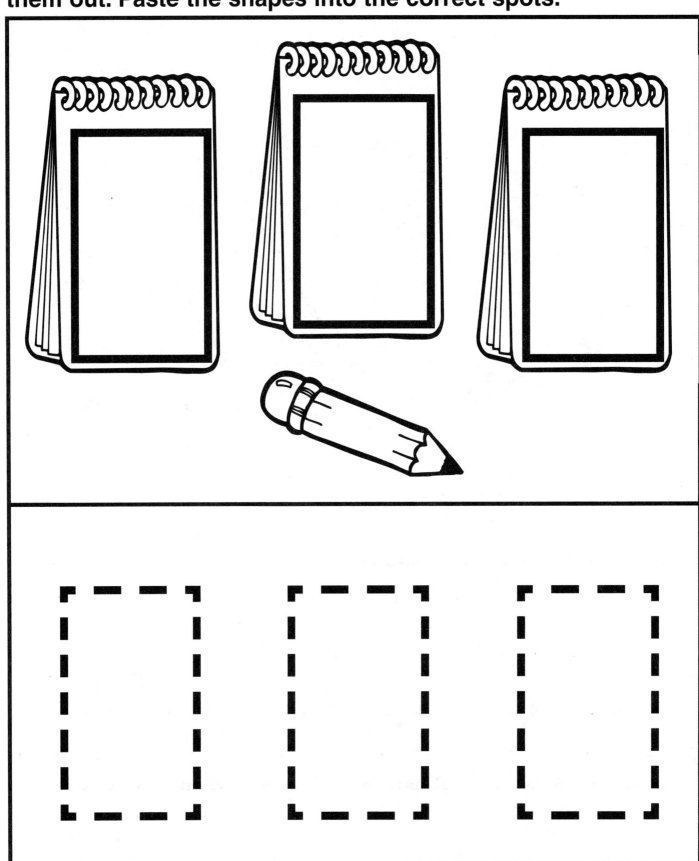

Preschool Basic Skills: Fine-Motor & Scissor Skills
© 2012 by Scholastic Teaching Resources

Name_____

Trace the shapes along the dotted lines. Color them and cut them out. Paste the shapes into the correct spots.

Preschool Basic Skills: Fine-Motor & Scissor Skills
© 2012 by Scholastic Teaching Resources

Name_____

Color the ladybugs. Cut out the ladybugs.